Introduction

Huck embroidery on monk's cloth. Is it easy? Engaging? Practical?

Yes, yes and yes!

Soft and knobby monk's cloth provides the perfect backdrop for charming patterns painted with yarn. This form of weaving is done on a large scale and is a first cousin to embroidery because it is an applied surface decoration. And it is a second cousin to cross-stitch because you use a charted design as a guide.

But this technique beats them both because the pattern takes shape quickly, and when the stitching is completed, you have a knockout throw (or afghan, or hot pad or pillow). And unlike embroidery and cross-stitch, mistakes are easy to correct.

I hope you enjoy these designs as much as I do. Happy weaving!

Trice Boerens

Meet the Designer

Trice Boerens has worked for many years in the quilting, needlework and paper industries. Along with designing projects for best-selling books and kits, she has also worked as a photo stylist, an art director and a creative editor.

The designs for this book were inspired by treasures that she uncovered in antique stores, flea markets and attics.

Table of Contents

Sea Glass Throw,
page 18

Sunny-Side–Up Runner,
page 34

Fall Garden Hot Pad,
page 12

General Instructions

The colorful patterns seen in this book are created with huck embroidery, or Swedish weaving, an ancient surface embroidery technique. Huck embroidery designs are created by weaving colored strands of yarn or other threads through the vertical raised threads occurring at regular intervals on the surface of even-weave fabrics like monk's cloth. This technique can be used to decorate everything from table runners to afghans.

The projects in this book include hot pads, throws, afghans, table runners and a pillow. They are all made with monk's cloth, a 100 percent cotton 4 thread x 4 thread basket-weave fabric available 60 inches wide in a variety of colors.

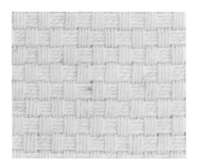

Preparing the Monk's Cloth
Monk's cloth quickly unravels if cut edges are not secured. When preparing the fabric for the projects in this book, always zigzag or serge all cut edges as instructed. Ease the fabric edges under the presser foot to prevent distortion.

For the throws and baby afghans, machine zigzag or serge along cut top and bottom edges. For the table runners, machine zigzag or serge around cut top, bottom and one side. For the pot holders and pillow, stitch around all four sides.

It is important to prewash monk's cloth because it can shrink up to 15 percent depending on whether the fabric is untreated, bleached or dyed. Preshrinking the fabric also helps hold the yarn in place by tightening the weave.

Machine wash with mild detergent in warm to hot water and dry completely. Always choose colorfast, washable yarn/thread for weaving on monk's cloth.

Be aware that even colorfast colors like red, purple and brown may release color when first washed. Just rinse the project in cold water to rid the project of excess dye.

Choosing & Cutting Yarn
For the patterns in this book, use worsted-weight and sport-weight yarns which work well on monk's cloth and match the weight of the fabric. Baby-weight yarns are usually too fine and get lost in the heavier monk's cloth threads.

Always choose a washable, colorfast yarn. Design density determines how much yarn is needed for each design.

Individual instructions will indicate how many lengths of yarn are needed to weave each row of a pattern. *A **length of yarn** is a piece of yarn equal to one width of your fabric (Figure 1)*. For example, if a pattern indicates two lengths of yarn for a row, cut a piece of yarn two times the width of the fabric piece being used.

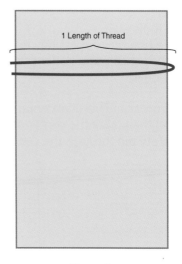

1 Length of Thread

Figure 1

When measuring yarn, do not stretch it, but allow it to lie across the fabric. Unless indicated otherwise, a single cut of yarn in the instructed length will be used to complete a row.

Needles

In huck embroidery, a large-eye, blunt-tip needle is used to insert the yarn/thread under the **floats**, *the strands of vertical threads in the even weave of the fabric weave.* Needles do not usually need to pierce the fabric.

Tapestry needles have blunt tips and come in a variety of sizes. A tapestry needle will easily slide under the floats when weaving. Use a size 13 tapestry needle for weaving monk's cloth.

A **bodkin** is a flat needle with a large eye used exclusively for stitching on monk's cloth. It may or may not have a bent tip. The eye is large enough to accept yarns.

Another needle that works well on monk's cloth is a **Susan Bates 5-inch steel weaving needle.** It is similar in size to the size 13 tapestry needle. Because of its length, you can make quick work of a row of stitching, especially when doing a significant number of straight stitches.

Weaving the Designs

• You will need the following basic sewing supplies and equipment to complete the projects in this book:

   Sewing machine in good working order
   General purpose thread in appropriate colors
   Hand-sewing needles and thimble
   Straight pins, safety pins and pincushion
   Seam ripper
   Measuring tools
   Iron, ironing board and pressing cloths
   Scissors: fabric shears and paper scissors
   Serger (optional)

• Find the horizontal and vertical centers of your fabric piece and then mark the center of the piece by placing a safety pin through the center float (Figure 2).

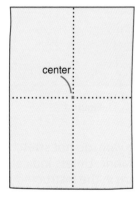

center

Figure 2

• Cut the yarn to the instructed length and thread the needle. Refer to the pattern for the starting point. If necessary, carefully count floats or measure to the position to begin weaving as indicated in the individual pattern instructions.

• Weave your length of thread through the center float as indicated in the pattern and draw up the yarn until the float is at the center of the length of thread (Figure 3).

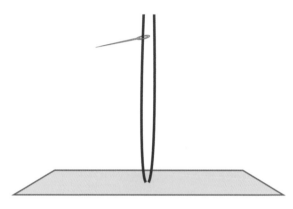

Figure 3

• Similar to drawing on an Etch A Sketch®, each length of yarn is worked from edge to edge with no breaks. Start weaving at the center of the fabric, repeating the design from the center out to the edge. Turn the fabric and chart upside down and work from the center out to the edge again. ***Note:*** *If you are right-handed, you will work from right to left. Left-handed weavers will work from left to right.*

• It is important to maintain an even tension while weaving. Use the Goldilocks rule of stitching, not too tight and not too loose. You will quickly get a feel for the correct tension after weaving two or three stitches in a row. Yarn should appear to be a part of the monk's cloth weave.

• Weave a set of design rows as instructed to complete a **design band**, *a set of rows that create a secondary design.* Then weave repeats across table runners, throws and afghans both above and below the center design band.

• Compare your work to the chart to prevent mistakes. But if mistakes do happen, correct small sections by working backward to remove your stitches until your weaving matches the chart and restitch the section.

To erase a row, snip the yarn every 2–3 inches and remove, being careful to cut only the yarn and not the threads that make up the monk's cloth.

• Secure the ends of each row by making one small stitch in the selvage edge and trim leaving a 3-inch tail. If there is no selvage edge, loop the yarn through the last float twice. **Note:** *Leave thread tails at ends of rows until design is correctly completed. If you do have to repair the design, having the thread tail will make it easier to reweave a row.*

Finishing Table Runners, Throws & Afghans

• When you have completed the design, machine zigzag-stitch along the **selvage**, *the bound lengthwise edge of the fabric*, using matching thread and a stitch that is small enough to catch the yarn tails in the stitching. Trim the yarn ends close to the stitching.

• To make a fringe on the narrow ends of throws and afghans, measure up from the cut edge the desired length of the fringe. Mark a stitching line with a removable fabric marker across the end, following a horizontal thread in the fabric. Machine zigzag along the marked line to secure the fringe ends. Carefully remove the horizontal or weft threads to make the fringe.

• For a more formal finished edge, cover the edges with a double-fold or French-fold binding. Cut 3-inch-wide coordinating fabric strips, either on the straight or bias fabric grain line, to equal the same length as the long side of the monk's cloth.

Stitch the fabric strips together if necessary on the short ends and press seams open. Trim to match length of monk's cloth side, adding 1 inch to the overall measurement if necessary.

Fold and press the short ends of the binding strip to the wrong side ½ inch. Then fold and press the strip in half lengthwise, wrong sides together.

Machine straight stitch the binding to the right side of the afghan or throw matching raw edges and using a ½-inch seam (Figure 4). **Note:** *You can also use a narrow, close zigzag-stitch.*

Fold the binding to the wrong side over the seam and pin in place from the front (Figure 5a). Stitch along the seam line from the right side catching the binding in the seam (Figure 5b).

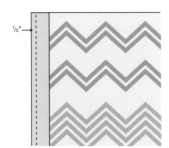

Figure 4

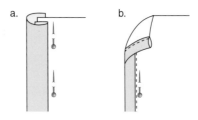

Figure 5

Huck Embroidery/Swedish Weaving Stitch Guide

Huck embroidery is a surface embellishment. The needle is used to weave thread/yarn under the **floats**, *the vertical threads of an even-weave fabric.* This keeps the thread/yarn on the right side of the fabric and makes it appear that the designs are actually part of the fabric weave.

The designs in this book are repeating designs made from very simple stitches. You repeat lines of stitching horizontally to create the designs.

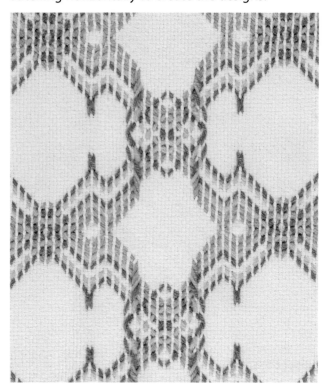

In the charts included in this book, the monk's cloth threads are represented by two rectangular sections. Floats are represented by two light gray vertical rectangles (Figure 6).

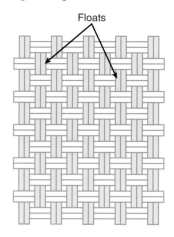

Figure 6

The chart also shows the colored threads woven through the floats and provides design center marks as well as where to begin stitching the repeat (shown by red or blue arrows) and spacing between design repeats (numbered rows). Charts also show numbered rows of each design.

Each chart shows at least one design repeat. Carefully follow each individual chart and count horizontal and vertical rows before stitching.

Instructions will refer to the following individual stitch diagrams that will make up the designs. ❖

Diagonal Running Stitch

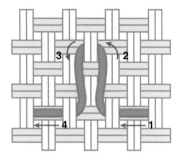

Open Loop Stitch

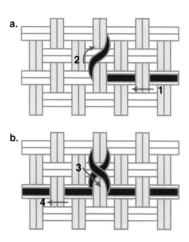

Twisted Loop Stitch

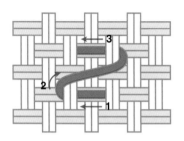

Diagonal Wrapping Stitch

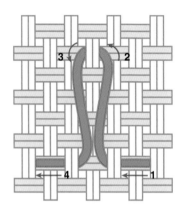

Open Loop Stitch (up two)

Twisted Loop Stitch (up two)

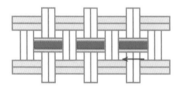

Straight Stitch

Slant Stitch

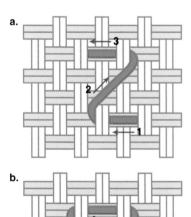

T Stitch

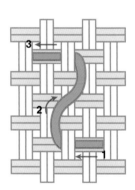

Slant Stitch (up two)

Citrusy Chevrons Hot Pad

Skill Level
Easy

Finished Size
10 x 10 inches

Materials
- 1 (15-inch) square, natural, preshrunk monk's cloth
- Worsted weight acrylic yarn*:
    #254 pumpkin
    #324 bright yellow
    #505 Aruba sea
    #624 tea leaf
- Tapestry needle
- 1 fat quarter turquoise print cotton fabric
- 2 (10½-inch) squares cotton batting
- 1 (10½-inch) square needle-punched insulated batting
- 1 package ½-inch plum single-fold bias tape
- All-purpose thread
- Embellishments (optional)
- Basic sewing supplies and equipment

Sample was made with Red Heart Super Saver yarn.

Pattern Notes
Begin stitching at the red arrow on the design chart as instructed.

All stitching is done right to left from the marked starting point. If left-handed, stitch from left to right from the marked starting point.

Refer to General Instructions and Huck Embroidery/Swedish Weaving Stitch Guide for fabric preparation, weaving techniques and individual stitch diagrams.

Thread Lengths
Cut two 48-inch lengths of each yarn color.

Stitches
This design uses the diagonal straight stitch and slant stitch (up two). Refer to the Huck Embroidery/Swedish Weaving Stitch Guide on page 6 for individual stitch diagrams.

Weaving the Design
1. Mark the horizontal and vertical center of the monk's cloth 15-inch square with a safety pin.

2. Referring to Citrusy Chevrons design chart on page 11, weave the tea leaf green yarn from the red arrow, marked one float up from the center, to the side edge.

3. Turn fabric and chart upside down and weave remaining yarn from red arrow to opposite edge to complete row 1 of design.

4. Refer to design chart for spacing and row color. Begin each row at blue arrow on chart to complete one design band of four rows.

5. Space design bands six floats apart. Stitch enough repeats to fill monk's cloth square.

Finishing the Hot Pad
Cutting

From turquoise print:
- Cut 4 (1½ x 13-inch) border strips.
- Cut 1 (11-inch) square for backing.

Stitch right sides together using a ¼-inch seam allowance unless otherwise indicated.

1. On wrong side of woven monk's cloth square, mark a 9½-inch square centered on design (Figure 1). Machine zigzag-stitch along marked line to stabilize fabric.

Figure 1

2. Trim 15-inch square to a 9½-inch square along stitching line, referring to Figure 1. Pin to mark center of each side.

3. Fold turquoise print border strips in half lengthwise and finger-press to mark center.

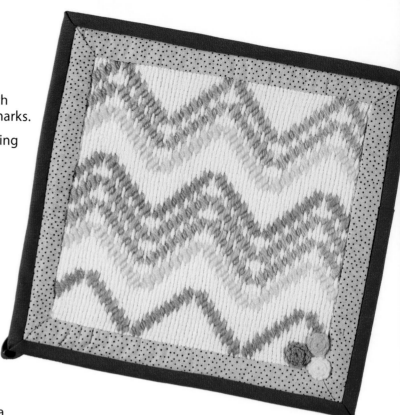

4. Position and pin border strips to monk's cloth square, right sides together, matching center marks.

5. Stitch borders to square, beginning and ending ¼ inch from all four square edges (Figure 2).

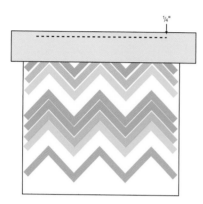

Figure 2

6. Fold and pin hot pad right sides together at a 45-degree angle on one corner (Figure 3). Place a straightedge along the fold and lightly mark a line across the border ends.

Figure 3

7. Stitch along the marked line, backstitching to secure. Trim seam to ¼ inch and press open (Figure 4). Press borders away from hot pad woven center creating a mitered border.

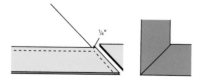

Figure 4

8. Layer turquoise print square, wrong side up; cotton batting; needle-punched insulated batting, shiny side down; a second cotton batting square and hot pad woven top, right side up. Pin in place.

9. Stitch in the ditch along border seams to hold layers together. Trim all edges even with hot pad top if necessary.

10. Stitch bias tape to top side of hot pad mitering corners. Turn bias tape to wrong side, pulling over the seam, and hand-stitch in place on hot pad back.

11. From remaining bias tape, cut one 6-inch strip. Fold in half lengthwise and stitch on both long edges. Fold strip in half to make a loop. Stitch loop to one corner on back.

12. Stitch embellishments to a corner as desired. ❖

Row 1

Citrusy Chevrons Hot Pad Chart
Note: *Segment repeat starts at red line.*

Fall Garden Hot Pad

Skill Level
Easy

Finished Size
9 x 9 inches

Materials
- 1 (12-inch) square, natural, preshrunk monk's cloth
- Worsted weight acrylic yarn*:
    #254 pumpkin
    #336 warm brown
- Tapestry needle
- 1 fat quarter orange solid cotton fabric
- 2 (9½-inch) squares cotton batting
- 1 (9½-inch) square needle-punched insulated batting
- 1 package ½-inch melon single-fold bias tape
- All-purpose thread
- Basic sewing supplies and equipment

Sample made with Red Heart Super Saver yarn.

Pattern Notes
Begin stitching at the red or blue arrows on the design chart as instructed.

All stitching is done right to left from the marked starting point. If left-handed, stitch from left to right from the marked starting point.

Refer to General Instructions and Huck Embroidery/ Swedish Weaving Stitch Guide for fabric preparation, weaving techniques and individual stitch diagrams.

Thread Lengths
Cut eight 42-inch lengths of each yarn color.

Stitches
This design uses the straight stitch, diagonal running stitch, twisted loop, and "T" stitch. Refer to the Huck Embroidery/Swedish Weaving Stitch Guide on page 6 for individual stitch diagrams.
Note: Some floats will have two strands of yarn woven through them as shown on the chart.

Weaving the Design
1. Find the horizontal and vertical centers of the monk's cloth 12-inch square and mark the square center with a safety pin.

2. Referring to Fall Garden design chart on page 14, begin weaving warm brown yarn through center float, marked with a red arrow, to the side edge.

3. Turn fabric and chart upside down and weave remaining yarn from center to opposite edge to complete row 1.

4. Begin row 2 at red arrow, referring to chart , weave a mirror image of row 1 using warm brown yarn to the side edge.

5. Turn fabric and chart upside down and weave remaining yarn from center to opposite edge mirroring row 1 to complete row 2.

6. Begin stitching row 3 at the blue arrow, spaced three floats above and one float to the left from the center float, in warm brown yarn. Repeat to weave row 4, referring to chart and completing one design band.

7. Begin stitching another design band in pumpkin yarn, spaced nine floats above the fabric center referring to steps 2–6.

8. Continue weaving design bands in alternating colors to fill the monk's cloth square.

Finishing the Hot Pad
Cutting
From orange solid:
- Cut 4 (1½ x 12½-inch) border strips.
- Cut 1 (10-inch) square for backing.

Assemble Hot Pad
Stitch right sides together using a ¼-inch seam allowance unless otherwise indicated.

1. On wrong side of woven monk's cloth square, mark an 8½-inch square centered on design (Figure 1). Machine zigzag-stitch along marked line to stabilize fabric.

2. Trim 12-inch square to an 8½-inch square along stitching line, referring to Figure 1. Pin mark center of each side.

3. Fold melon print border strips in half lengthwise and finger-press to mark center.

4. Position and pin border strips to monk's cloth square, right sides together, matching center marks.

5. Stitch borders to square, beginning and ending ¼ inch from all four square edges (Figure 2).

Figure 1

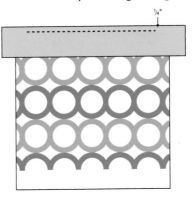

¼"

Figure 2

6. Fold and pin hot pad right sides together at a 45-degree angle on one corner (Figure 3). Place a straightedge along the fold and lightly mark a line across the border ends.

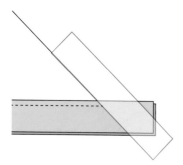

Figure 3

7. Stitch along the marked line, backstitching to secure. Trim seam to ¼ inch and press open (Figure 4). Press borders away from hot pad woven center.

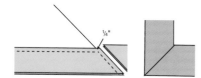

Figure 4

8. Layer orange solid square, wrong side up; cotton batting; needle-punched insulated batting, shiny side down; a second cotton batting square and hot pad woven top, right side up. Pin in place.

9. Stitch in the ditch along border seams to hold layers together. Trim all edges even with hot pad top if necessary.

10. Stitch bias tape to top side of hot pad mitering corners. Turn bias tape to wrong side,

pulling over the seam, and hand-stitch in place on hot pad back.

11. From remaining bias tape, cut one 6-inch strip. Fold in half lengthwise and stitch on both long edges. Fold strip in half to make a loop. Stitch loop to one corner on back. ❖

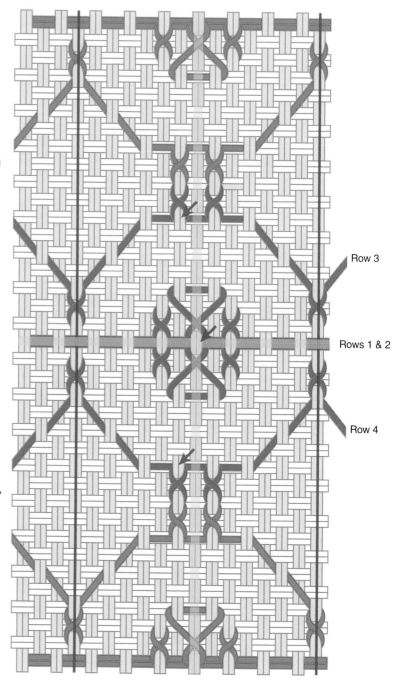

Row 3

Rows 1 & 2

Row 4

Fall Garden Hot Pad Chart
Note: Segment repeat starts at red line.

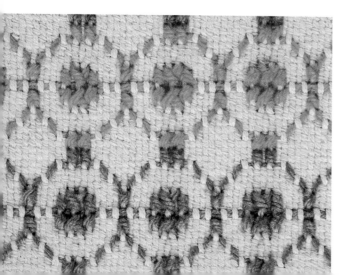

Bow Tie Pillow

Skill Level
Intermediate

Finished Size
12 x 16 inches

Materials
- 1 (18 x 22-inch) rectangle preshrunk white monk's cloth
- Worsted weight acrylic yarn*:
    #254 pumpkin
    #324 bright yellow
    #624 tea leaf
- Tapestry needle
- 1 fat quarter coordinating cotton print or solid
- 1 (12 x 16-inch) pillow form
- All-purpose thread
- Basic sewing supplies and equipment

Sample made with Red Heart Super Saver yarn.

Pattern Notes
Begin stitching at the red or blue arrows on the design chart as instructed.

All stitching is done right to left from the marked starting point. If left-handed, stitch from left to right from the marked starting point.

Refer to General Instructions and Huck Embroidery/ Swedish Weaving Stitch Guide for fabric preparation, weaving techniques and individual stitch diagrams.

Thread Lengths
Cut the following yarn lengths for color indicated:

tea leaf	9 (4 length) pieces
bright yellow	10 pieces (varying lengths; longest at 4 lengths)
pumpkin	10 pieces (varying lengths; longest at 2 lengths)

Stitches

This design uses the straight stitch, diagonal running stitch, diagonal wrapping stitch, slant stitch and slant stitch (up two). Refer to the Huck Embroidery/Swedish Weaving Stitch Guide on page 6 for individual stitch diagrams. *Note: Some floats will have two strands of yarn woven through them as shown on the chart.*

Weaving the Design

1. Find the horizontal and vertical centers of the monk's cloth 18 x 22-inch rectangle and mark the rectangle center with a safety pin.

2. Referring to Bow Tie design chart on page 17, weave tea leaf yarn through center float, marked with a red arrow, to the side edge.

3. Turn fabric and chart upside down and weave remaining yarn from center to opposite edge to complete row 1.

4. Referring to chart on page 17, count six floats up and six floats to the right of the center float and weave a second tea leaf bow tie row. Repeat, staggering tea leaf bow tie rows to cover the monk's cloth rectangle.

5. Weave bright yellow rows diagonally across the rectangle. Begin weaving at the blue arrow on the chart, seven floats up and one to the right of the center float.

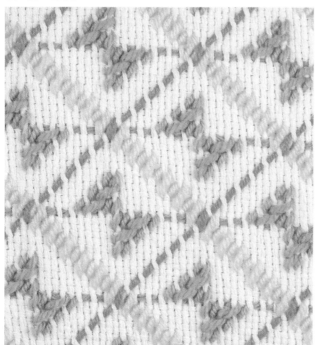

6. Turn fabric upside down and weave remaining yarn from center to opposite edge to complete row 2. Refer to chart and weave remaining rows.

7. Weave row 3 diagonally across the rectangle. Begin weaving at the blue arrow. Weave to the side, turn fabric and chart upside down and weave to the opposite side to complete the row. Refer to the chart for spacing and weave remaining rows to cover the rectangle.

Finishing the Pillow

Cutting

From fat quarter:

- Cut 1 (13 x 17-inch) rectangle for pillow back.

Assemble Pillow

Stitch right sides together using a ¼-inch seam allowance unless otherwise indicated.

1. On wrong side of woven monk's cloth rectangle, center and mark a 12 x 16-inch rectangle. Machine-zigzag along marked line to stabilize fabric.

2. Trim monk's cloth rectangle to 13 x 17 inches.

3. Pin and stitch backing to monk's cloth rectangle and stitch along 12 x 16-inch marked lines, leaving a 6-inch opening on one long side for turning.

4. Trim seam allowances to ½ inch and finish with a zigzag stitch, overedge stitch or serger. Trim corners at an angle.

5. Turn right-side out, gently pushing corners out. Insert pillow form.

6. Turn opening seam allowances to inside and hand-stitch together using a slipstitch or ladder stitch to complete the pillow. ❖

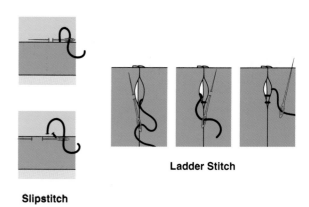

Ladder Stitch

Slipstitch

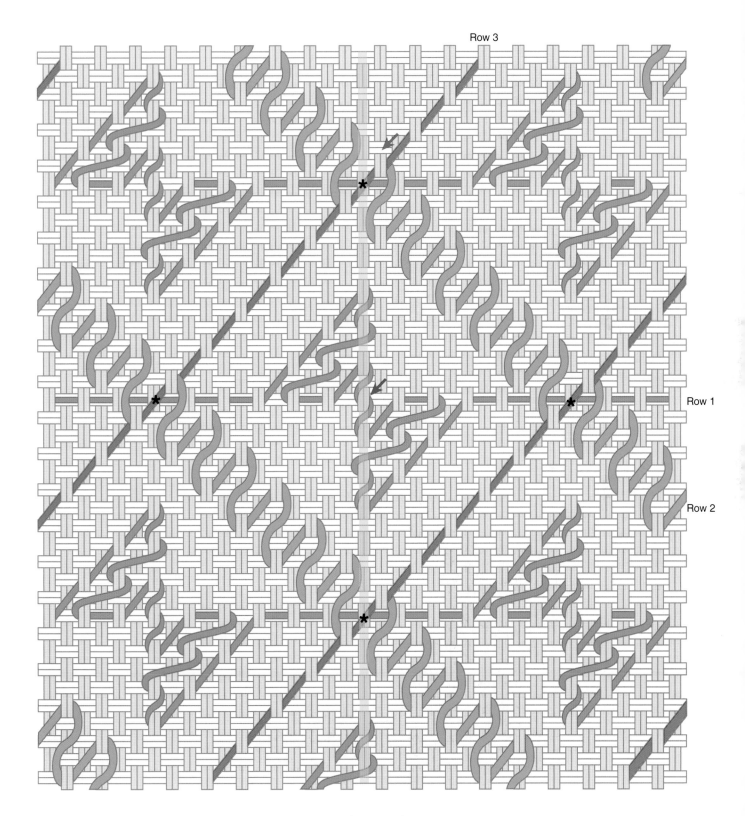

Row 3

Row 1

Row 2

Bow Tie Pillow Chart
Note: Asterisks indicate diagonal stitch. Refer to stitch diagrams on page 7.

Sea Glass Throw

Skill Level
Easy

Finished Size
48 x 76 inches

Materials
- 2½ yards preshrunk white monk's cloth
- Worsted weight acrylic yarn*:
    #505 Aruba sea
    #668 honeydew
    #336 warm brown
- Tapestry needle
- Coordinating double- or French-fold binding (purchased or self-made)
- All-purpose thread
- Basic sewing supplies and equipment
Sample was made with Red Heart Super Saver yarn.

Pattern Notes
Begin stitching at the red or blue arrows on the design chart as instructed.

All stitching is done right to left from the marked starting point. If left-handed, stitch from left to right from the marked starting point.

Refer to General Instructions and Huck Embroidery/Swedish Weaving Stitch Guide for fabric preparation, weaving techniques and individual stitch diagrams.

Thread Lengths
Cut the following yarn lengths for color indicated for each design band. You will weave 11 design bands for a 48 x 76-inch throw:

Aruba sea	4 (2½ length) pieces
honeydew	4 (2½ length) pieces
warm brown	4 (2½ length) pieces

Stitches
This design uses the diagonal running stitch, slant stitch (up two), and twisted loop (up two) stitch. Refer to the Huck Embroidery/Swedish Weaving Stitch Guide on page 6 for individual stitch diagrams. ***Note:** Some floats will have two strands of yarn woven through them as shown on the chart.*

Weaving & Finishing the Throw
1. Find the horizontal and vertical centers of the monk's cloth yardage and mark the center with a safety pin.

2. Referring to Sea Glass Chart A on page 22, begin weaving honeydew yarn at red arrow to the side edge.

3. Turn fabric and chart upside down and weave remaining yarn from center to opposite edge to complete row 1.

4. Turn fabric and chart right-side up and count one float up from center. Begin weaving row 2 with warm brown yarn, repeating row 1. Refer to Figure 1 to weave the needle under each slant stitch (up two) combining the rows to create a twisted appearance.

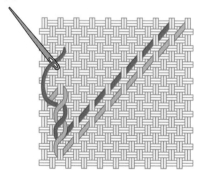

Figure 1

5. Turn fabric and chart upside down and weave to opposite side completing row 2. Continue weaving rows 3–5 in the same manner.

6. Turn fabric and chart right-side up. Count down one float from red arrow and weave row 6 referring to chart to complete design band.

7. Turn Chart A upside down. Count up one float from center. Begin weaving row 1 using honeydew yarn at red arrow, referring to steps 2 and 3, to complete row 1. Weave rows 2–5, referring to steps 4 and 5, to create overlapping rows with first design band as shown in Figure 2 on page 20.

8. Referring to Sea Glass Chart B on page 23, count down seven floats from row 6 twisted loop and begin weaving row 6 from blue arrow on chart to opposite edge using warm brown yarn.

20

Figure 2
Note: Asterisks indicate overlapping threads in next repeats.

9. Turn fabric and chart upside down and weave remaining yarn from blue arrow to opposite edge.

10. Weave remaining 11 rows to complete a second design band referring to steps 2–6.

11. Repeat steps 2–9 to complete 11 design bands.

12. Finish throw edges as desired, referring to Finishing Table Runners, Throws & Afghans on page 5 in the General Instructions to complete the throw. ❖

Weaving Wisdom

Although this design seems complex, it is very easy to execute. Of the 12 rows that make up a design band, 10 are the same repeat; refer to rows 1–5 on Chart A.

The remaining two rows, labeled row 6 on Chart A, add a lacy accent to the windows that are created by yarn overlays that can be seen in Figure 2.

Row 5
Row 4
Row 3
Row 2
Row 1
Row 6

Sea Glass Throw Chart
Chart A
Note: Segment repeat starts at red line.

Sea Glass Throw Chart
Chart B

Flame Stitch Runner

Skill Level
Easy

Finished Size
22 x 78 inches, excluding fringe

Materials
- 2⅜ yards 44/45-inch-wide unbleached, preshrunk muslin
- 2½ yards preshrunk natural monk's cloth
- Worsted weight acrylic yarn*:
  - #668 honeydew
  - #528 medium purple
  - #579 pale plum
  - #254 pumpkin
- Tapestry needle
- Coordinating double- or French-fold binding, purchased or self-made (optional)
- All-purpose thread
- Basic sewing supplies and equipment

Sample made with Red Heart Super Saver yarn.

Pattern Notes
Begin stitching at the red or blue arrows on the design chart as instructed.

All stitching is done right to left from the marked starting point. If left-handed, stitch from left to right from the marked starting point.

Refer to General Instructions and Huck Embroidery/ Swedish Weaving Stitch Guide for fabric preparation, weaving techniques and individual stitch diagrams.

Thread Lengths
Cut the following yarn lengths of color indicated for each design band:

honeydew	1 (5 length) piece
medium purple	1 (3 length) piece
pale plum	2 (5 length) pieces
pumpkin	3 (5 length) pieces

Stitches
This design uses the diagonal running stitch, slant stitch (up two) and twisted loop stitch (up two).

Refer to the Huck Embroidery/ Swedish Weaving Stitch Guide on page 6 for individual stitch diagrams.

Weaving the Design
1. Cut the monk's cloth yardage in half lengthwise making two 30 x 90-inch rectangles. Refer to Preparing the Monk's Cloth on page 3 in the General Instructions. Set aside one rectangle for another project after preparing both rectangles for weaving.

> ### Weaving Wisdom
> To straighten the edges of any even-weave fabric or to cut a larger piece into smaller pieces, just pull a horizontal or vertical thread from the weave.
>
> Zigzag-stitch along the missing thread to secure the edge, and then trim if you will be working more with the fabric piece.

2. Find the horizontal and vertical center rows of the monk's cloth rectangle and mark the center of the runner with a safety pin.

3. Referring to Flame Stitch Chart A (top half) on page 27, begin weaving row 1 with honeydew yarn at red arrow to side edge.

4. Turn fabric and chart upside down and weave remaining yarn from center to opposite edge to complete row 1.

5. Referring to Flame Stitch Chart A (top half), count down three floats from red arrow and weave row 2 using pale plum yarn to side edge.

6. Turn fabric and chart upside down and weave remaining yarn from center to opposite edge to complete row 2.

7. Repeat steps 5 and 6 with pumpkin yarn to complete row 3.

8. Refer to Chart A (top and bottom half) on pages 27 and 28, to weave rows 4–7 paying close attention to spacing and yarn color. Begin weaving rows at blue arrows in colors indicated on chart to complete a design band.

Cowgirl Throw Chart
Chart A
Note: *Segment repeat starts at red line.*

Cowgirl Throw Chart
Chart B

Sunny-Side–Up Runner

Skill Level
Intermediate

Finished Size
22 x 78 inches, excluding fringe

Materials
- 2⅜ yards 44/45-inch-wide unbleached muslin
- 2½ yards natural monk's cloth
- Worsted weight acrylic yarn*:
    #324 bright yellow
    #505 Aruba sea
    #385 royal blue
- Tapestry needle
- All-purpose thread
- Basic sewing supplies and equipment

*Red Heart Super Saver yarn

Pattern Notes
Begin stitching at the red or blue arrows on the design chart as instructed.

All stitching is done right to left from the marked starting point. If left-handed, stitch from left to right from the marked starting point.

Refer to General Instructions and Huck Embroidery/Swedish Weaving Stitch Guide for fabric preparation, weaving techniques and individual stitch diagrams.

Thread Lengths
Cut the following yarn lengths of color indicated for each design band:

Aruba sea   4 (3½ length) pieces

royal blue   2 (3½ length) pieces

Cut the following yarn lengths of color indicated for each flower center:

bright yellow   13 (18-inch) pieces

Stitches
This design uses the running stitch, diagonal running stitch, slant stitch (up two), twisted loop and twisted loop stitch (up two).

Refer to the Huck Embroidery/Swedish Weaving Stitch Guide on page 6 for individual stitch diagrams.

Weaving the Design
1. Cut the monk's cloth yardage in half lengthwise making two 30 x 90-inch rectangles. Refer to Preparing the Monk's Cloth on page 3 in the General Instructions. Set aside one rectangle for another project after preparing both rectangles for weaving.

Weaving Wisdom
To straighten the edges of any even-weave fabric or to cut a larger piece into smaller pieces, just pull a horizontal or vertical thread from the weave.

Zigzag-stitch along the missing thread to secure the edge, and then trim if you will be working more with the fabric piece.

2. Find the horizontal and vertical center rows of the monk's cloth rectangle and mark the center of the runner with a safety pin.

3. Referring to Chart A on page 38, begin weaving row 1 with royal blue yarn at red arrow to side edge.

4. Turn fabric and chart upside down and weave remaining yarn from center to opposite edge to complete row 1.

5. Refer to Chart A and weave row 2 beginning at the blue arrow using Aruba sea yarn to side edge.

6. Turn fabric and chart upside down and weave remaining yarn from center to opposite edge to complete row 2.

7. Weave row 3, beginning one float above the blue arrow and mirroring row 2, to complete a design band.

8. Turn chart upside down and repeat steps 3–7 to create the center medallion design band as shown in Figure 1 on page 36.

9. Weave six medallion design bands above the center design band 8½ floats apart and staggered. Repeat below the center band.

10. When 13 medallion design bands are completed, add a flower to the center of each medallion.

Figure 1

11. Mark center of medallion. Referring to Chart B on page 38, begin weaving at red arrow leaving a 3-inch yarn tail. Weave as indicated using figure eight (one up) and figure eight (two up) stitches as shown in Chart B. Trim yarn ends to about ½ inch to complete the flower.

12. Repeat step 11 to weave a flower in the center of each medallion.

Finishing the Runner
Cutting

From muslin:
• Cut 1 (22 x 74-inch) rectangle for runner backing.

Assembly
Stitch right sides together using a ½-inch seam allowance unless otherwise indicated. The following instructions will make a 22 x 78-inch bed runner with a 2-inch fringe on the short ends.

1. Measure and mark 37 and 39 inches from the horizontal center row of the woven monk's cloth to one short end.

2. Zigzag-stitch along the 37-inch mark to secure the runner end.

3. Trim along the horizontal row at the 39-inch mark. Remove the horizontal threads from the monk's cloth up to the zigzag stitching to make the fringe.

Weaving Wisdom

If finishing a project with a fringe, always remember to zigzag-stitch along the top edges of the fringe areas to stop your afghan or runner from unraveling too much.
Fringing can be done on all four sides of a project. Just be sure to zigzag-stitch across the design row ends to anchor both the monk's cloth and the yarn. Use a narrow stitch width that will catch the yarn tails in the stitching
Always create your fringes first and then finish any other edges as desired.

4. Repeat steps 1–3 on the opposite end of the runner.

5. Measure and mark the vertical row 23 inches from the vertical center of the woven monk's cloth to one long side of the runner. Zigzag-stitch or serge along this vertical row to secure the runner edge and trim.

6. Repeat on opposite long edge of runner and set aside.

7. Hem short ends of runner backing with a ¼-inch double turned hem; press hem flat.

Weaving Wisdom

To make a double turned hem, press the width of the hem to the wrong side. Press again, the width of the hem, to the wrong side, placing the cut edge inside the fold.
Stitch together along the first folded edge to secure the hem.

8. With right sides together, pin the backing rectangle to the woven runner, matching the long sides and the backing short ends to the top of the fringe at zigzag stitching. Stitch long edges together.

Note: The backing is not the same width as the woven runner.

9. Turn right sides out, center backing, and press edges flat. *Note: Because the backing is not the same width as the runner, runner edges should turn to the back when backing is centered. This means the backing will not show on the right side when placed on your bed.*

10. Hand-stitch the short backing ends to the back of the runner to complete. ❖

Weaving Wisdom

A unique feature to this project is a free-standing center flower added to the center of the medallions made by two mirroring design bands.

This could be added to any huck embroidery design with a similar open area, giving it a Mediterranean tile feeling.

Sunny-Side–Up Runner
Chart A
Note: *Segment repeat starts at red line.*

Row 3

Row 2

Row 1

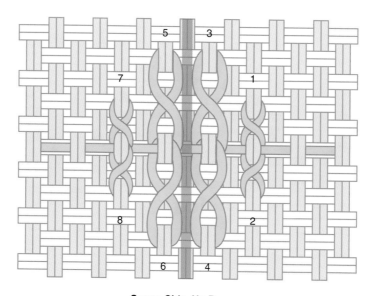

Sunny-Side–Up Runner
Chart B
Flower Center

Dresden Plates Baby Afghan

Skill Level
Easy

Finished Size
48 x 60 inches

Materials
- 2 yards preshrunk natural monk's cloth
- Worsted weight acrylic yarn*:
    #08879 sky
    #53223 grass
    #00608 bright yellow
- Tapestry needle
- Coordinating double- or French-fold binding, purchased or self-made (optional)
- All-purpose thread
- Basic sewing supplies and equipment

Sample made with Bernat Super Value yarn.

Pattern Notes
Begin stitching at the red or blue arrows on the design chart as instructed.

All stitching is done right to left from the marked starting point. If left-handed, stitch from left to right from the marked starting point.

Refer to General Instructions and Huck Embroidery/Swedish Weaving Stitch Guide for fabric preparation, weaving techniques and individual stitch diagrams.

Thread Lengths
Cut the following yarn lengths of color indicated for each design band:

sky   4 (3½ length) pieces

Cut the following yarn lengths of color indicated for each contrasting design row:

bright yellow   19 (2½ length) pieces

Cut the following yarn lengths of color indicated for each running stitch band:

grass   3 (1½ length) pieces

Stitches

This design uses the straight stitch, diagonal running stitch, slant stitch (up two) and twisted loop (up two). Refer to the Huck Embroidery/Swedish Weaving Stitch Guide on page 6 for individual stitch diagrams. *Note: Some floats will have two strands of yarn woven through them as shown on the chart.*

Weaving & Finishing the Afghan

1. Find the horizontal and vertical center rows of the monk's cloth yardage and mark the center of the afghan with a safety pin.

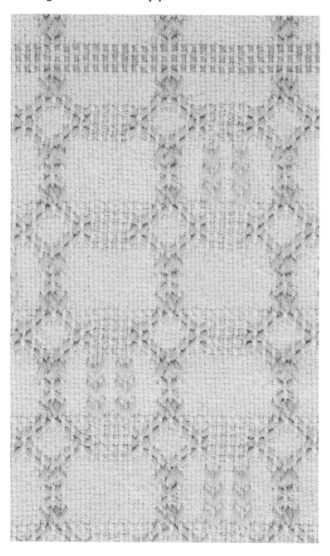

2. Referring to Dresden Plates Chart A on page 41, begin weaving row 1 using sky yarn at red arrow to side edge.

3. Turn fabric and chart upside down and weave remaining yarn from center to opposite edge to complete row 1. Refer to Chart A for spacing and weave remaining three rows of the design band.

4. Space design bands eight floats apart, referring again to Chart A, and weave six design bands to create a design block. *Note: Design bands are eight floats apart at centers and meet at points.*

5. Referring to Chart B on page 42, begin weaving row 1 of the running stitch design band with grass yarn at the blue arrow to side edge.

6. Turn fabric and chart upside down and weave remaining yarn from center to opposite edge, completing row 1.

7. Refer to Chart B for spacing and weave remaining two rows of running stitch design band.

8. Weave 2½ Dresden plate design bands below the running stitch design band referring again to Chart B for spacing.

9. Repeat steps 5–8 on the opposite side of the design block.

10. Yellow accent rows are woven into every third plate shape created by the Dresden plate design bands as shown in Figure 1.

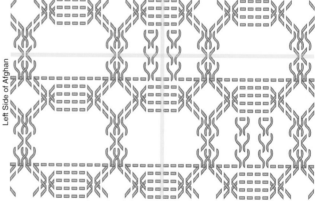

Figure 1

11. Referring to Dresden Plates Chart C on page 43, weave bright yellow accent row from blue arrow to side edge.

12. Turn fabric and chart upside down and weave remaining yarn from center to opposite edge to complete the bright yellow accent row.

13. Complete weaving the yellow accent rows in the same manner to every third plate shape formed by the Dresden plate design band.

14. Finish afghan edges as desired referring to Finishing Table Runners, Throws & Afghans on page 5 in the General Instructions to complete the throw. ❖

Weaving Wisdom

The Dresden plate pattern includes a four-row repeat that creates the plate design when woven next to each other and a one-row accent design that is seen in every third plate.

The Dresden plate pattern is broken up on the afghan by four running-stitch design bands.

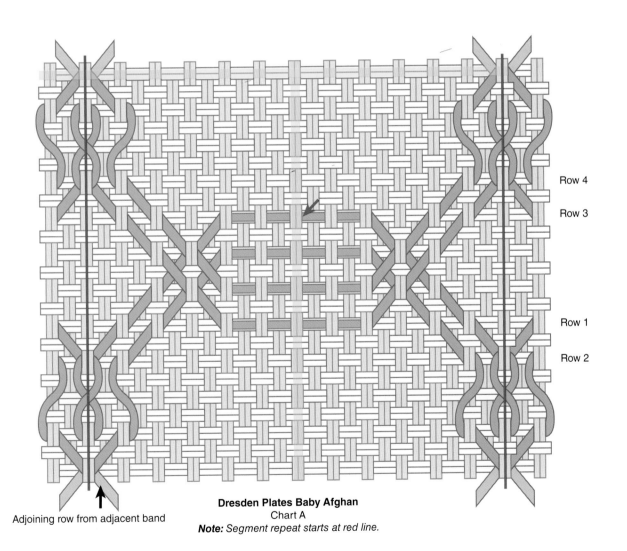

Row 4

Row 3

Row 1

Row 2

Adjoining row from adjacent band

Dresden Plates Baby Afghan
Chart A
Note: Segment repeat starts at red line.

Dresden Plates Baby Afghan
Chart B

Dresden Plates Baby Afghan
Chart C

Rose Trellis Afghan

Skill Level
Easy

Finished Size
48 x 60 inches

Materials
- 2 yards preshrunk white monk's cloth
- Worsted weight acrylic yarn*:
    #55415 princess
    #53223 grass
- Tapestry needle
- Coordinating double- or French-fold binding, purchased or self-made (optional)
- All-purpose thread
- Basic sewing supplies and equipment

Sample made with Waverly for Bernat (princess) and Bernat Super Value (grass) yarns.

Pattern Notes
Begin stitching at the red or blue arrows on the design chart as instructed.

All stitching is done right to left from the marked starting point. If left-handed, stitch from left to right from the marked starting point.

Refer to General Instructions and Huck Embroidery/ Swedish Weaving Stitch Guide for fabric preparation, weaving techniques and individual stitch diagrams.

Thread Lengths
Cut the following yarn lengths for color indicated for each design band:

princess	2 (3 length) pieces
grass	2 (3 length) pieces

Cut the following yarn lengths for color indicated for each contrasting design band:

grass	2 (4 length) pieces
	2 (3 length) pieces

Stitches
This design uses the straight stitch, diagonal running stitch, twisted loop stitch, twisted loop stitch (up two), "T" stitch, open loop stitch, and open loop stitch (up two). Refer to the Huck Embroidery/Swedish Weaving Stitch Guide on page 6 for individual stitch diagrams. ***Note:*** *Some floats will have two strands of yarn woven through them as shown on the chart.*

Weaving & Finishing the Afghan
1. Find the horizontal and vertical center rows of the monk's cloth yardage and mark the center with a safety pin.

2. Referring to Rose Trellis Chart A on page 46, begin weaving princess yarn at red arrow to the side edge.

3. Turn fabric and chart upside down and weave remaining yarn from center to opposite edge to complete row 1.

4. Begin weaving grass yarn at red arrow on Chart A repeating steps 2 and 3 to complete row 3.

5. Turn fabric and chart upside down and begin weaving princess yarn at blue arrow referring again to Chart A. Weave rows 2 and 4 completing a design band.

6. Weave seven design bands, staggering the rose trellis designs to create a design block.

7. Weave rows 1–3 to the top of the design block. Turn the fabric upside down and repeat on the opposite end of the design block.

8. Referring to Rose Trellis Chart B on page 47, count down six rows from trellis point and weave row 1 using grass yarn from center to side edge. Turn fabric and chart upside down and weave remaining yarn from center to opposite edge.

9. Turn fabric and chart right-side up and weave row 3 referring to the chart.

10. Turn the fabric and chart upside down and repeat steps 8 and 9 to weave rows 2 and 4 of the contrasting band.

11. Weave a contrasting band on the opposite end of the design block, repeating steps 8–10.

12. Referring to Rose Trellis Chart A, weave eight additional design bands on both ends of the design block.

13. Finish throw edges as desired, referring to Finishing Table Runners, Throws & Afghans on page 5 in the General Instructions to complete the throw. ❖

Weaving Wisdom

The rose trellis pattern is woven in design bands, making up a design block that is broken up by two contrasting design bands.

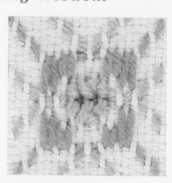

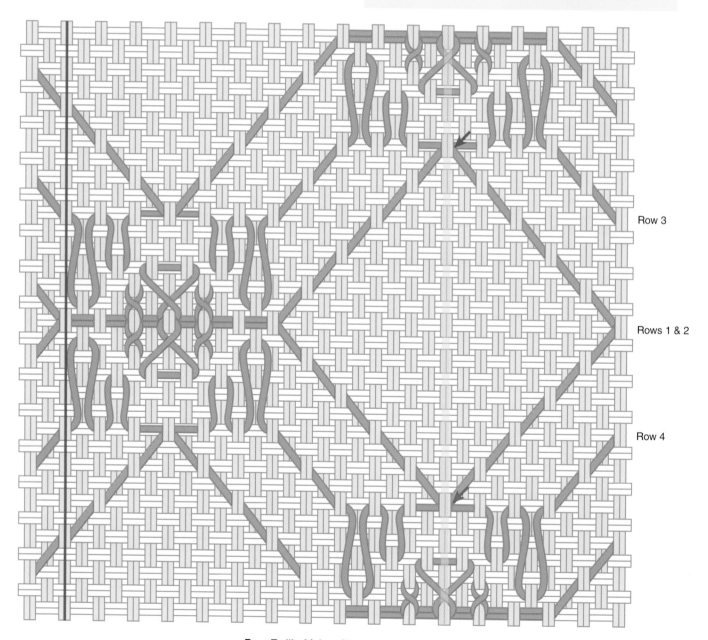

Row 3

Rows 1 & 2

Row 4

Rose Trellis Afghan Chart
Chart A
Note: Segment repeat starts at red line.

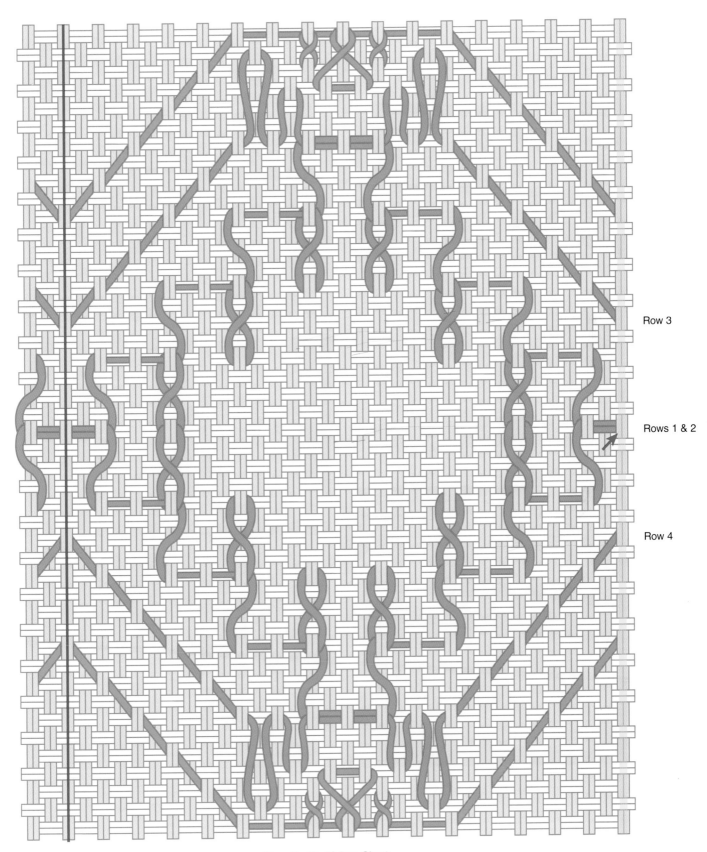

Row 3

Rows 1 & 2

Row 4

Rose Trellis Afghan Chart
Chart B
Note: *Segment repeat starts at red line.*

Photo Index

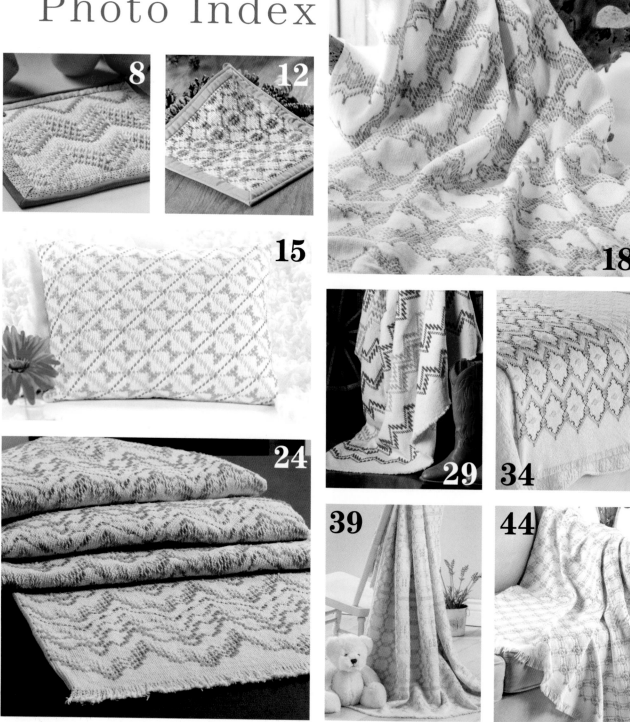

8

12

15

18

24

29

34

39

44

Annie's® *Learn Huck Embroidery on Monk's Cloth* is published by Annie's, 306 East Parr Road, Berne, IN 46711. Printed in USA. Copyright © 2014, 2017 Annie's. All rights reserved. This publication may not be reproduced in part or in whole without written permission from the publisher.

RETAIL STORES: If you would like to carry this pattern book or any other Annie's publication, visit AnniesWSL.com.

Every effort has been made to ensure that the instructions in this pattern book are complete and accurate. We cannot, however, take responsibility for human error, typographical mistakes or variations in individual work. Please visit AnniesCustomerCare.com to check for pattern updates.

ISBN: 978-1-57367-364-8
56789